MW01259962

Mata Ortiz Pottery Today

Guy Berger

Schiffer Publishing Ltd

Acknowledgments

Attempting any project like this involves many talented people. I would like to acknowledge and thank the following people for helping me along the way. Without them I would still be procrastinating, sorting through the pictures and information, and who knows when it would have been completed?

My heartfelt thanks to my wife, Daniela, who continues to put up with me on our life journey together; she is truly my best friend.

Thank you to my lovely daughter, Diana, for helping me read, re-read, correct the text and be, at times, like my high school English teacher.

Thanks to my son, Peter, who made many good suggestions (the best of which was to go off by myself somewhere where I could concentrate on the project) and for his help organizing the photo shoot.

I thank Thena Garoufes for her tremendous effort in organizing and adding captions to close to 1000 photographs so we could select and present them in a comprehensive form. Denise Antonio also helped to sort and organize the pictures.

I thank Karen Kuehn for her unique photography style and for taking the time to make sure we had just the right shots to include. Most of the photographs were expertly taken by Karen.

My thanks also go to Enso Medici who helped organize the pottery for pictures and also helped us sort through the photos for caption and price information and also Tony Weber and David Archuleta who all assisted us on the days we took all the pictures.

Thanks to my friend Steve Rose, who has answered dozens of my questions about Mata Ortiz, the pottery, and the potters with his vast knowledge and good-natured humor. I also thank Steve for providing photographs from the village of Mata Ortiz. And to Nancy Schiffer, for her continued confidence in me to get the project completed satisfactorily.

Finally, I express sincere gratitude to Spencer MacCallum for taking time to read the draft and make essential contributions and corrections.

Other Schiffer Books by Guy Berger:
Pueblo Pottery Families, with Lillian Peaster, ISBN:978-0-7643-2880-0. $19.95
Pueblo and Navajo Comtemporary Pottery & Directory of Artists, with Nancy Schiffer, ISBN:978-0-7643-1896-9. $29.99

Copyright © 2010 by Guy Berger
Pottery photographs © 2010 by Karen Kuehn
Other photographs © 2010 by Steve Rose

Library of Congress Control Number: 2010930020

All rights reserved. No part of this work may be reproduced or used in any form or by any means—graphic, electronic, or mechanical, including photocopying or information storage and retrieval systems—without written permission from the publisher.

The scanning, uploading and distribution of this book or any part thereof via the Internet or via any other means without the permission of the publisher is illegal and punishable by law. Please purchase only authorized editions and do not participate in or encourage the electronic piracy of copyrighted materials.

"Schiffer," "Schiffer Publishing Ltd. & Design," and the "Design of pen and inkwell" are registered trademarks of Schiffer Publishing Ltd.

Cover and book designed by: Bruce Waters
Type set in Zurich Lt.

ISBN: 978-0-7643-3470-2
Printed in China

Schiffer Books are available at special discounts for bulk purchases for sales promotions or premiums. Special editions, including personalized covers, corporate imprints, and excerpts can be created in large quantities for special needs. For more information contact the publisher:

Published by Schiffer Publishing Ltd.
4880 Lower Valley Road
Atglen, PA 19310
Phone: (610) 593-1777; Fax: (610) 593-2002
E-mail: Info@schifferbooks.com

For the largest selection of fine reference books on this and related subjects, please visit our web site at
www.schifferbooks.com
We are always looking for people to write books on new and related subjects. If you have an idea for a book please contact us at the above address.

This book may be purchased from the publisher.
Include $5.00 for shipping.
Please try your bookstore first.
You may write for a free catalog.

In Europe, Schiffer books are distributed by
Bushwood Books
6 Marksbury Ave.
Kew Gardens
Surrey TW9 4JF England
Phone: 44 (0) 20 8392 8585; Fax: 44 (0) 20 8392 9876
E-mail: info@bushwoodbooks.co.uk
Website: www.bushwoodbooks.co.uk

Contents

Introduction

It has been a special pleasure to witness the modern evolution of Mata Ortiz pottery as we have bought and sold thousands of pieces over the past 15 years. I can remember my brother, Greg Berger, buying various pots made in Mexico when he ran Las Palmas Import Company many years ago. Unless the pottery was made by famous potter and originator of the Mata Ortiz pottery style Juan Quezada or his protégés, the pottery we were seeing at that time was elementary at best.

The resurrection of pottery making in northern Mexico began from the time Juan Quezada discovered ancient pottery shards as a boy near the Paquimé ruins to the time he re-discovered the Paquimé pottery-making methods. "By trial and error he discovered every step in the process of making ceramics: how to prepare the clay, adding coarser material such as sand to temper or strengthen it; how to form a pot (una olla) from a flat circle of clay.......he discovered how to grind specific minerals and mix paint.....and after much experimentation he settled on a method of firing each pot individually."

Since then, there has been a tremendous increase in the quality and quantity of the pottery we are buying from Mata Ortiz, Mexico. In virtually every category, whether the pottery style is polished black, black on black, matte black, polychrome, new more colorful pots, or miniatures, the craftsmanship has improved every year.

You'll see for yourself, as you browse through the pictures in this book, how far the art form has come. Around 1955, Juan Quezada found pottery shards in the hills above Mata Ortiz. He developed over time, with much trial and error, the process to reproduce clay pottery from that area. Juan's generosity in mentoring not only his immediate family in the pottery making techniques but many other budding potters in his village allowed the art to flourish. We estimate there are upwards of 350 potters in and around the village now. The fine work of over 110 of them is showcased here.

This book is organized into six sections. The first part explores similarities in the bird motifs of Native American Pueblo pottery and modern Mata Ortiz designs. The next five sections are grouped by pottery style: black, polychrome, sgraffito (etched) designs, brightly colored pots, and finally special shapes. My intention is to enhance the readers' enjoyment by paying close attention to design details through the years, enabling them to judge similarities among the art forms. I would also like to challenge the reader to discover other similarities among Native American and Mata Ortiz pottery, and to hypothesize how the symbols came to be so similar.

I hope this look into the contemporary pottery from Mata Ortiz enhances your appreciation of the fine work being done by so many talented Mexican potters. As the pottery continues to expand in both form and expression, my hope is that this book will mark an important milestone in the road that helps us follow the progress of this precious art.

Famed potter and originator of Mata Ortiz pottery, Juan Quezada, has been named a national treasure by the Mexican government.

We see new shapes, designs and colors almost every time we buy new merchandise. There seems to be much experimentation with clay, texture, paint and shapes, as every artist seeks to find their very own niche. This creates an element of curiosity and excitement in our store, as new merchandise encourages our staff to educate our customers and share our enthusiasm for Mata Ortiz pottery.

The intrinsic value and collectibility of Mata Ortiz pottery is on the rise. My recommendation is that any serious collectors consider a few pieces of this exceptional pottery for their collection.

Children fishing in the Rio Palanganas

Similarities in Design
The Mata Ortiz - Acoma Pueblo Connection

Having been involved in buying and selling Native American pottery for the past twenty years, my eye instantly recognizes how many of the designs from Mata Ortiz and Acoma Pueblo resemble each other. The most common design similarity among Paquimé, Acoma, and Mata Ortiz pottery is the bird. Exploring the sometimes subtle, sometimes striking similarities between ancient Paquimé pottery examples, modern Native American Acoma Pueblo pottery and modern Mata Ortiz designs was a fascinating exercise for me.

Paquimé was an old village in northern Mexico that existed from the years 1200-1450 AD, very near the modern day village of Mata Ortiz. Acoma Pueblo sits 50 miles west of Albuquerque, in New Mexico.

Paquimé ruins. Original construction was from rammed adobe. Adobe brick was donated and the prehistoric site was partially renovated.

These structures were used to house parrots at the prehistoric Paquimé ruins.

It is known that the Paquimé people raised macaws. There are stories handed down about Acoma Pueblo people following parrot-like birds to find water. I believe there is strong evidence for correlating the designs of the two places. Many contemporary Mata Ortiz pottery patterns also depict this most interesting bird.

Paquimé people created pottery unique to their part of the world and decorated the pottery with designs from things in their world. "In many aspects Paquimé looks like a Southwestern Pueblo, with multistory adobe room blocks bordering communal plazas and pottery that is clearly part of the Southwestern polychrome tradition. In other ways, Casas Grandes is an enigma. Ball courts, monumental architecture, a stratified social hierarchy, macaw breeding, and ceramic effigies all suggest Mesoamerican influences." (Powell, M., *Secrets of Casas Grandes*) This reference to macaw breeding could help explain the designs found on pottery shards among the Paquimé ruins.

It is also known that "parrots and macaws were depicted in Mimbres pottery as early as 1000 AD. The Museum of Indian Arts and Culture has a display of Parrot Skeletons (dated at around 1300 AD) and macaw skeletons (dated at around 1000 AD), which were found in New Mexico. The feathers of parrots and macaws were prized for their beauty and often used in dances and ceremonies." (Susman, N.) In fact, many photos of stylized bird designs on historic pottery are found in the book *Secrets of Casas Grandes*.

The bird motif was done in many different varieties, but has the same basic design. Some are easy to spot, while others take a while to see within the entire pattern. Most bird patterns have a semi-circle ending in a point, signifying a beak. As you follow the curves around it is noticeable that there is a light dot surrounded by darker lines to represent an eye.

This is evident on Acoma pots with stylized bird designs as well. Some pots showed even further development of the bird, with abstract feather designs for both wing and tail feathers.

Were the designs I was seeing on the Mexican pottery connected to the New Mexico Pueblo pottery? How did the figures come to be so alike? How did the ideas transfer through Mesoamerica? As I looked at these unique similarities, I wondered how the designs came to take on some of the same characteristics, yet be separated by time and great distances. Could it be that the "Acoma Parrot" and the "Paquimé macaw" is one and the same? Were these the same birds in a story told to me by Barbara Cerno, a well known Acoma potter, about elder Acoma ladies following colorful birds each morning in order to find water? What other ways could the design have traveled through Mesoamerica?

Comparison of Acoma parrot design by Tina Garcia (left) and a multi-design, etched bird pattern pot by Luís Armando Rodríguez Mora (right).

The bird design is carried on in many of the modern examples of Mata Ortiz pottery, and I find it most interesting how close these macaw designs are to the bird motifs used at Acoma Pueblo, New Mexico. My hypothesis is that the bird designs used by modern Mata Ortiz potters are taken from the old Paquimé examples, so there could be a correlation among Paquimé bird designs, Acoma Pueblo designs, and modern Mata Ortiz designs.

Comparison of Acoma parrot design by Emma Lewis (left) and buff polished pot with beige bird and traditional patterns and designs (right) by Rodrigo Pérez. 11" h. x 9" d.

Comparison of Acoma parrot design by Franklin Peters (left) and traditional and bird designs by Rodrigo Pérez.

Firing Black Pottery

1. Covering the unfired pots

2. Placing firewood for an even heat

3. Starting the fire

4. Winding down the fire

5. Uncovering the pots

6. The finished product

Black

There is nothing quite like the black pottery that is made at Mata Ortiz. They have polishes you can literally see yourself in polishes so magnificent you need a second opinion to make you believe its clay you're looking at and not some type of high-tech metal.

The high luster of Mata Ortiz pots was discovered accidentally by Macario Ortiz, when he found a shiny black mark made by pencil lead after he fired a pot. He introduced the graphite technique that is widely used in the village to this day, using a combination of photocopier toner (containing graphite) mixed with diesel fuel that is applied with a rag or a sponge. This mixture, much like a clay slip, can be left alone for a dull matte finish, or polished with a smooth stone for a mirror-like finish. The polished graphite pot is shiny even before it is fired, enabling the contemporary artist to experiment with painting vivid colors on their pots before firing.

The technique used to create these unique black pots is called "reduction firing" (see previous page), in which cow manure, cottonwood bark or split wood is used as fuel to fire the pottery. Iron oxides, present in most clays and normally red or brown in color, turn black by a chemical reaction when heated in the absence of oxygen. The resulting clay becomes black throughout, not just on the surface.

Oxidation firing, on the other hand, allows the clay to retain its natural color and mineral paints are applied to the surface. Graphite is such a colorant. Others are red, from iron oxides, blue or green, from copper oxides, and black, from manganese. Unlike clay from the American Southwest, Mata Ortiz colorants contain no organic ingredients.

Many of the black Mata Ortiz pots in the following photographs have matte-finish black designs painted over the polished surface. This is accomplished by painting over the pre-polished pot with the same graphite-diesel mixture, applied with a human-hair brush. Some potters also use a combination of matte paint design with corrugated indentations in various patterns, such as circles and triangles. There are also pieces that use only the indented technique to create beautiful patterns. All the designs are well balanced and expertly painted. You will see the potters' creativity expressed in unique designs as part of three-dimensional figures and shapes. Some pots have lizards protruding from them while others have polished melon ridges, are shaped like turtles and fish, or exhibit sculpted heads of wildlife.

It is a testament to the increasing skill of the potters that we are drawn to the shapes and designs on the black pottery. We tend to forget how well each piece is constructed. The pots are delicate to the touch and fascinating to the eye. I still marvel at the talent each artist possesses to be able to create such beautiful works of art.

Black polished pot with thick painted designs and square, flared rim. Signed Jaime Quezada. 9 ½"h x 9"d.

Black on black polished pot with detailed designs. Signed Eduardo Ortiz. 7 7/8"h x 5 ¾"d.

Black gunmetal polish, swirled melon pot. Signed Eduardo Ortiz. 5 ½"h x 6 ¼"d.

Black on black polished pot with detailed designs. Signed Eduardo Ortiz. 5 ½"h x 5 ¼"d.

Black polished seed pot with patterns around the rim. Signed Martha M de Quezada. 1 ¾"h x 3 ¾"d.

Black polished vase with melon style bottom and painted neck. Signed Tavo Silveira. 6 ½"h x 4 ¾"d.

Tavo Silveira pottery

Tavo Silveira

Tavo Silveira and family.

Tall black on black polished vase with wide neck and painted designs. Signed Luz Elva Ramírez. 10"h x 6 3/8"d.

Black on black polished pot with painted patterns exterior and interior rim. Signed Eduardo Ortiz. 8 ½"h x 8"d.

Black on black polished pot with painted designs. Signed Eduardo Ortiz. 10 ½"h x 9"d.

Black on black polished pot with textured bottom and detailed, finely painted top. Signed Susy D. Martínez. 7"h x 8 ¾"d.

Black on black polished pot with concave sides and painted designs. Signed Eduardo Ortiz. 7 ½"h x 7"d.

Black on black polished pot with traditional painted designs. Signed Virginia Salvador Baca. 4 ¼"h x 4 ¾"d.

Black on black polished pot with traditional designs. Signed Paty Rodríguez. 4 ½"h x 4"d.

Black polished vase with textured bottom and long black on black neck. Signed Suzy D. Martínez. 8"h x 5"d.

Large pot with gunmetal finish. Signed P. Carona. 8 ¾"h x 9 ½"d.

Melon style pot with gunmetal finish. Signed José M. Macino. 5 ½"h x 5"d.

Black on black polished wedding vase with traditional patterns. Signed Oscar G. Quezada, Jr. 8"h x 6 ½"d.

Black on black polished pot with traditional patterns. Signed Oscar. G. Quezada Jr. 7"h x 6 ½"d.

Black polished pot with punched handles and square corrugated rim. Signed Oscar G. Quezada Jr.. 5 ½"h x 6 ½"d.

Black on Black polished pot with traditional patterns and flattened sides. Signed Abigail López. 5"h x 4"d.

Black polished pot with raised matte snake. Signed Pedro Quezada. 4 ½"h x 4 1/2"d.

Black on black polished pot with painted patterns. Signed Oscar G Quezada Jr.. 4 ½"h x 4 ½"d.

Black on black polished seed pot with painted designs. Signed Martha M. de Quezada. 3 ½"h x 4"d.

Black polished flat pot with corrugated surface. Signed Mariano Quezada. 3 ¼"h x 8 ¾"d.

Black on black polished pot with traditional patterns and turtle-shaped opening. 2"h x 4 ½"d.

Small polished pot with traditional patterns. Signed RRR. 1 ¾"h x 1 ½"d.

Small black on black polished pot with traditional patterns. Signed Maizi Rios. 2 ½"h x 2"d.

Large black polished bowl with corrugated surface interior and exterior. Signed Reynaldo Quezada. 5 ¾"h x 15"diameter.

Black on black polished pot with raised snake on the surface. Signed Martha M. de Quezada. 5 ¾"h x 6"d.

Black gunmetal, melon style pot, with matte clay-formed bear heads at the rim. Signed Héctor Ortega. 10"h x 7"d.

Potter Héctor Ortega – known for his black pottery with large animal heads.

Black polished pot with traditional patterns and raised matted lizards on the surface.
Signed Reynaldo Quezada. 6 ½"h x 10"d.

Black polished pot with clay protrusions from the surface representing the shape of a turtle. Signed Jaime Quezada. 6 ½"h x 8 ½"d.

Black polished pot contoured from the interior and painted with traditional designs. Signed Consolación Quezada. 9 ½"h x 10 ½"d.

Black gunmetal, melon style pot with matte clay formed eagle heads at the rim. Signed Héctor Ortega. 9 ¾"h x 7"d.

Black matte corrugated pot with small polished rim and handles. Signed Tito Tena. 3″h x 4 ½″d.

Black polished effigy style pot with frog head at top. Signed Paty Quezada. 4 5/8"h x 4 ¼"d.

Black matte corrugated seed jar with polished rim. Signed Tito Tena. 3 ¾"h x 4"d.

Black polished pot with corrugated exterior and square, etched opening. Signed Mariano Quezada. 7"h x 7"d.

Black polished egg shaped seed pot with formed lizard over top. Signed Olivia Domínguez. 2 ¾"h x 2 ¾"d.

Black polished effigy style pot with formed owl head at top. Signed Paty Quezada. 4 ½"h x 4 ½"d.

Black polished effigy fish pot. Signed Paty Quezada. 3"h x 5 ½"d.

Polychrome

People have mentioned in the past couple of years how impressed they are with the quality of the potting and designs in Mata Ortiz polychrome pottery. Many have asked me to give them a sense of the progress these fine artists have made. Whether it is the thin walls, the intricate design, the "feel" of a pot or the meaning of a particular design, they are always impressed.

The move away from quantity toward a renewed emphasis on quality over the past decade has been a boon to both the potters and the traders who represent their work. Traders have taught their clients over the years what to look for in quality Native American pottery. Their tips include looking for pieces with good shapes and sharp designs. Today they emphasize the same aspects with Mexican pots. We advise our collectors to seek superior quality to enhance their collections.

It continues to impress me that the Mata Ortiz potters are not bound to any particular design, as are many of the Native American potters. Native potters use very similar designs in most cases, rarely venturing far from the traditional designs. The Mexican potters, however, stay with designs they have developed over years of practice but also tend to experiment. Mata Ortiz artists create not only innovative designs but are adept at unique shapes as well.

Mixed clay vase with traditional red and black designs and wide, flarind rim. Signed Rodrigo Ponce. 7" h. x 6 1/2" d.

Beige seed pot with large painted feather pattern filled diamond designs in red and brown. Signed Blanca Quezada. 5" h. x 6 1/2" d.

As you browse through the photos of Mata Ortiz polychrome pots, notice how varied the designs have become. Although many of the patterns are similar to what has been done in the past, there is considerable innovation in design today. For example, you see on many of the "eye dazzler" pots an additional pattern to break up the design, yet keep it perfectly balanced. Even in more simple geometric patterns, the painter pays particular attention to making the design pleasing to the most discriminating eye.

Variations in Mata Ortiz polychrome designs are numerous. We see incredibly fine designs made possible by the brushes invented by Juan Quezada, made from the clippings of children's hair. There are differences in clay color and mixtures of various clays that give the pots a marbled look. Mirror images grace many of the pots, showing an exact replication of design on both sides. Combinations of colors with mixtures of matte (dull) finish and polished finish make patterns jump out at the viewer. There are also pots with relief patterns (designs cut deeply into the body of the pot) carved into the finish and then decorated. Many facets of design are present in the following examples, such as intricate geometric panels, human figures, animals, feathers and lightning.

Buff polished pot with red and black traditional patterns. Signed Mireya Quezada. 8"h x 6 ¼"d.

Buff polished pot with thick painted rows of red and black square, geometric patterns. Signed Ernesto Arras Olivas. 9 3/8"h x 8"d.

Buff polished pot with red and black checker pattern. Signed Sara Corona. 6 ½"h x 5 ¾"d.

Black on buff polished pot with bowman, quail and geometric patterns. Signed Diana Loya. 6 3/8"h x 6"d.

Red matte pot with heavy beige geometric patterns. Signed Rodrigo Pérez. 5"h x 5 5/8"d.

Buff polished pot with large red square and black checker patterns. Signed Ernesto Arras Olivas. 9"h x 8"d.

Mixed clay vase with traditional red and brown patterns. Unsigned. 5 ½"h x 4"d.

Buff polished pot with green and black traditional patterns. Signed Ana Veloz C. 4 7/8"h x 4"d.

Buff polished pot with red and black water serpent and traditional patterns. Signed Zulema Quezada. 5 ½"h x 4 ¼"d.

Buff polished pot with red and black detailed designs. Signed Blanca Quezada. 5 ¼"h x 5 ¾"d.

Green matte vase with orange, red and black traditional patterns and square, flared rim. Signed Ramón Villa. 6 5/8"h x 5"d.

Buff polished pot with full red and black geometric designs. Signed Israel Rentería Heras. 5 ¼"h x 6 ½"d.

Buff polished pot with red and black criss-cross pattern and painted rim. Signed Efrén Ledezma. 5 ¼"h x 4 5/8"d.

Carmen Veloz & her husband, Jesús Veloz

Buff polished pot with detailed red and black checker/star pattern. Signed Carmen Veloz. 2 5/8"h x 4"d.

Red matte pot with traditional black and white patterns. Signed Oscar G Quezada, Jr. 5"h x 4 3/8"d.

Terracotta polished pot with black and red checker/diamond pattern. Signed Carmen Veloz. 5 1/4"h x 7 1/2"d.

Red matte pot with black checkered, diagonal oval designs. Signed Carlos Loya. 5 ¾"h x 9"d.

Black matte pot with traditional red and white patterns. Signed Oscar G Quezada, Jr. 9 ½"h x 6"d.

Buff pot with black and red checkered, diagonal oval designs. Signed Edgar Flores. 5"h x 6"d.

Red matte pot with traditional black and white patterns. Signed Oscar G Quezada, Jr. 7"h x 6 ½"d.

Red matte pot with traditional black and white patterns. Signed Martha M de Quezada. 11 ¼"h x 8 ½"d.

Day of the Dead, Dia de los Muertos. Signed Javier Martínez Méndez. 8"h x 6"d.

Mixed clay pot with black and red traditional designs. Signed Oscar G Quezada, Jr. 6 ½"h x 6 ½"d.

Buff polished pot with black and red traditional and bird head patterns with wide flat rim. Signed Roberto Bañuelos. 8 ¾"h x 10 ½"d.

Buff polished wedding vase with traditional red and black patterns and fish design. Signed Cristina Acosta Teresa Jáquez. 8 ½"h x 7'd.

Tan polished wedding vase with leaf and diamond pattern and fish painted on handle. Signed Gerardo Ledezma Veloz. 8"h x 6 ½"d.

Buff polished pot with red dimensional, fineline pattern. Signed Alfredo "Freddy" Rodríguez. 6"h x 6 ½"d.

Buff polished pot with diagonal red and brown checker pattern. Signed Karina Gallegos. 4"h x 4 ½"d.

Red matte pot with simple, traditional beige painted patterns. Signed Israel Rentería Heras. 11 ¾"h x 9"d.

Light terracotta polished pot with beige traditional patterns and designs. Signed Rodrigo Pérez. 10 ¾"h x 9"d.

Black matte bowl with beige and red traditional patterns painted interior and exterior. Signed Octavio González. 4 ½"h x 13"diameter.

Buff polished bowl with red and black traditional patterns painted interior.
Signed Octavio González. 3"h x 12"diameter.

Red polished pot with full black checker design and square, flared rim.
Signed Yoly Ledezma. 4 ¾"h x 8"d.

Red matte pot with traditional beige painted designs. Signed Octavio Pérez. 7 ½"h x 6 ½"d.

Red polished pot with traditional black designs. Signed Ismael Flores. 4 ¾"h x 5 ¾"d.

Buff polished pot with red and black detailed medallion pattern. Signed Israel Rentería Heras. 3 ½"h x 5 ½"d.

Brown matte pot with traditional beige and pink patterns. Signed Martha M de Quezada. 4 ½"h x 5"d.

Red polished pot with checker pattern painted with ants, and
square flared rim. Signed Yoly Ledezma. 4"h x 5"d.

Red seed pot with white pattern around rim.
Signed Octavio González. 4"h x 6"d.

Light terracotta polished vase with thick beige checker and diamond pattern and step pattern rim. Signed Rubén Ponce. 6 ½"h x 5 ¾"d.

Beige vase with red and brown checker style pattern and slanted, step cut rim. Signed Ernesto Arras Olivas. 7 ¼"h x 7"d.

Black matte vase with red and white traditional patterns. Signed Silvia Silveira. 7"h x 5 7/8"d.

Potter Silvia (Lila) Silveira.

Terracotta polished pot with black and red lizard and traditional designs.
Signed Manuel Glez (González). 6 ¼"h x 6 ½"d.

Brown matte vase with pink and beige traditional patterns. Signed Martha M de Quezada. 5"h x 4 ½"d.

Buff polished pot with red and brown repetitive geometric patterns. Signed Karina Gallegos. 6"h x 4 ¼"d.

Speckled tan pot with orange and black patterns. Signed Yolanda Pedregón. 4"h x 4 ½"d.

Buff polished pot with red and black traditional patterns. Signed Olivia Domínguez. 4 ½"h x 3 ¼"d.

Mixed clay seed pot with black and red lizard and traditional patterns. Signed Elena Mora. 2 ¾"h x 4 ¼"d.

Red polished seed pot with beige patterns. Signed Ángel Amaya. 3 ½"h x 4 ½"d.

Red polished pot with black design. Signed Julio Ledezma. 7 ½"h x 11 ¾"d.

Red polished wedding vase with black and red checker pattern and squared rims and handle. Signed Elsa Ledezma, Jorge Ponce. 4 ½"h x 4"d.

Red polished pot with black fish and traditional designs. Signed César Bugarini. 13 ¾"h x 11"d.

Terracotta matte pot with traditional red and white patterns. Signed Nicolás Quezada. 15 ¾"t x 10 ½".

Small buff polished wedding vase with red and black checker pattern and painted turtle on handle. Unsigned. 3 ½"h x 2 ¼"d.

Speckled red pot with black lizards. Signed Yolanda Pedregón. 3 ½"h x 4 ¾"d.

Beige polished pot with red and black fish and traditional patterns. Signed Ana Veloz. 4 ½"h x 4 ½"d.

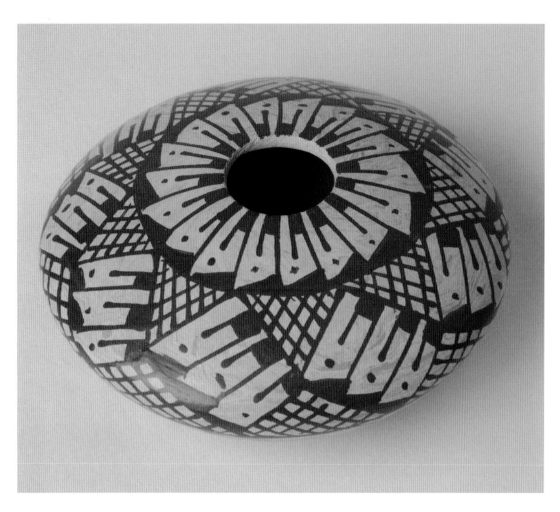

Mixed clay seed pot with traditional red feather designs. Unsigned. 1 ½"h x 2 ¾"d.

Terracotta matte pot with red and black patterns. Signed Karin Camacho. 1 ¾"h x 2 ¾"d.

Buff seed pot with Carmen's painted signature lizard. Signed Carmen Veloz. 1 ½"h x 2 ¾"d.

Tan polished plate with rabbit and brown and red patterns. Signed Blanca Quezada. 5"diameter.

Small terracotta vase with black and red lizard and patterns. Signed Karin Camacho. 3"h x 1 ¾"d.

Beige egg shaped seed pot with painted insects in yellow, green, orange and red.
Signed Yoly Ledezma. 2 ½"h x 2 ¼"d.

Beige polished seed pot with red and black fish. Signed Raúl Jurado Domínguez.
1"h x 2"d.

Buff polished pot with thick red and and black geometric checker patterns.
Signed Karina Gallegos. 2"h x 3"d.

Small red polished vase with black checker pattern. Signed Guadalupe Ledezma Quezada. 3 ½"h x 3 ½"d.

Tan polished pot with brown and red turtles.
Signed José Andrés Villalba H. 5 ¾"diameter.

Beige polished pot with painted black geometric and hunters patterns, and etched parrot head. Signed Luís Armando Rodríguez. 5 ¾"h x 6 ½"d.

Buff polished pot with black designs and raised red lizard. Signed Olivia Domínguez Rentería. 5"h x 4 ½"d.

Red pot with traditional beige patterns and slanted and step-cut rim. Signed Martha M de Quezada. 7 ½"h x 4 5/8"d.

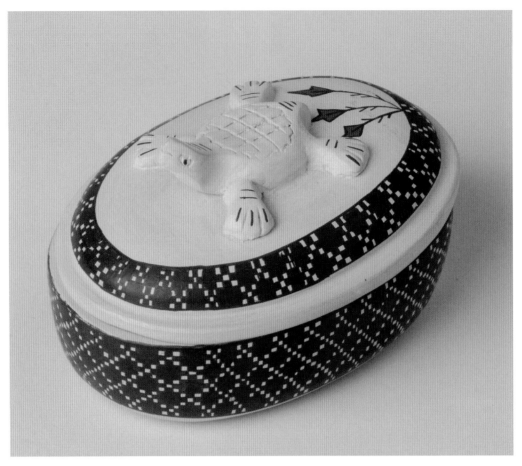

Buff polished box painted with black painted patterns and raised turtle lid.
Signed Amelia Martínez. 3"h x 4 ¼"d.

Buff polished pot with green and black checker pattern and imprinted pattern around rim.
Signed María Acosta. 2 ½"h x 5"d.

Buff polished pot with red and black serpent design and detailed, formed handles. Signed Gerardo and Norma Tena. 5 ½"h x 6"d.

Buff polished pot with black dimensional designs and red crocodile and turtle patterns. Signed Alfredo Rodríguez. 4 ¾"h x 5 7/8"d.

Brown matte pot with traditional red and white patterns. Signed Octavio González. 11"h x 8 ½"d.

Buff polished pot with black geometric patterns. Signed Luís Armando Rodríguez Mendez. 6 ½"h x 5 ¼"d.

Sgraffito or Etched

Mata Ortiz pottery that is decorated by etching the surface of the pot to expose a different color underneath is a style that has grown steadily over the past ten years. Today, we see more and more pottery done in this fashion. Decorating the pottery using this method, sometimes called sgraffito, enables the artist to be even more creative with new designs. These fine pots are sometimes broad, detailed, whimsical and always interesting. Some of this pottery tells a story, with various animals frolicking on the surfaces and intricate designs that leave you with the question, "How do they do this?"

Designs that are cut into the surface of a pot can be large or small and cause the pattern to become almost three-dimensional. Potters who use this style must be expert painters and adept at using a knife or other type of blade.

Some scenes are carved into pots that are fired in one color, then the artist removes pieces of the surface a little at a time to unveil the intended designs. Other scenes are created by painting a lighter surface with a darker design, then very delicately cutting away small amounts of the surface to enhance the picture. An example of this style follows.

Some of my favorite examples are the pots that combine two or more colors, enabling the artist to create a masterpiece using different colors to contrast different parts of the design. A good example of this technique is the pot with birds sitting in a tree. Notice the wonderful detail that makes the birds come alive. This delicate scratching of the surface gives the birds depth and can be seen in many other contemporary Mata Ortiz pots.

Above and opposite: Beige pot with detailed icised and sgraffitoed red, black and yellow bird designs. Signed Ricardo Delgado Cruz. 10" h. x 6 1/2" d.

Red impressed clay pot with large square, notched opening. Signed Reynaldo Quezada. 6 ¼"h x 10 ½"d.

Red polished wedding vase with black etched lizards. Signed Adriano Bañuelos. 6 ¾"h x 5"d.

Buff pot etched with black raccoon and scallop patterns. Signed Irma Trevizo. 6 ¾"h x 5 ½"d.

Buff polished vase with detailed, etched parrots and traditional patterns accented in green, red and black.
Signed Lupita Quezada. 6 ½"h x 5"d.

Buff polished pot with detailed, etched fish, lizards and water serpent. Signed Eduardo Olivas Quintana. 6"h x 6 ½"d.

Buff polished pot with detailed and colored Madonna. Signed Luís Almeraz. 7"h x 5 ½"d.

Light terracotta polished pot with detailed and etched ravens and fish accented in black and red.
Signed Heribario Armando Arras Olivas. 7"h x 6 ½"d.

Leonel Lopez

Red polished pot with black etched lizards. Signed
Leonel López Saenz. 8 ¼"h x 9"d. $

Beige polished pot with detailed, etched red and black mimbres fish and traditional patterns.
Signed Eduardo Olivas Quintana. 6 ¼"h x 6 ½"d.

Tan bowl with detailed, etched turtles and swordfish painted in green, black, blue and red.
Signed Ramiro Veloz Casas. 2 ¾"h x 9"diameter.

Tan bowl with detailed, etched parrots, lizards, rabbit, fish and quail painted in green, black, blue and red.
Signed Ramiro Veloz Casas.

Black pot with etched dragonflies. Signed Celia Ortega. 4 ¾"h x 3 ¾"d.

Black pot with white etched horse and scallop patterns. Signed Karin Camacho. 6"h x 4 ½'d.

Black pot with white etched frogs.
Signed Claudia Veloz. 2 ½"h x 4"d.

Black pot with white etched butterflies. Signed Claudia D. Veloz.
3 ¾"h x 2 ½"d.

Black polished vase with white etched lizards and step cut neck. Signed Elicena Cota. 3 ¾"h x 2 ½"d.

Large, buff polished pot completely etched and painted with various birds, lizards and fish patterns in red, green and black with a large, asymmetrical opening. Signed Martín Olivas Quintana. 10 ¼"h x 8 ½"d.

Color

Since the discovery of the graphite polish technique in the 1980s, there have been numerous innovations in Mata Ortiz pots that contain bright, interesting colors. Most of the early pottery examples were decorated with the traditional colors of red, created with iron oxides, and shades of black, made from manganese.

Black polished pot with incised and colored butterfly design. Signed Karen Camacho. 2 3/4" h. x 4" d.

Pot with gunmetal polish with red, white, and green traditional patterns. Signed Anastasio Villalobo. 8" h. x 7 1/2" d.

The polished graphite pots from Mata Ortiz are shiny even before they are fired. This enables the artists to apply colored designs directly onto the polished surface before the pot is fired. To achieve this effect, the pots featuring color are fired to allow oxygen to circulate during the process (oxidation firing). According to Steve Rose, a resident of Mata Ortiz, the color the artists put on the multi-colored pots sometimes look the same before and after firing, but not always. He states, "I once was with Eli Navarette when he pulled a pot out of the smoldering dung fire; I couldn't believe he attempted this at such high temperature, and thought it would almost certainly explode. It was nightfall, so the pot was actually glowing red with no design visible, but as he set it down on the cement floor and it began to cool, the colors of the paint began changing. It wasn't until the piece was fully cooled that you could see all of Eli's incredible animal designs come to life."

Beige dish with incised and painted turtles and swordfish. Signed Ramiro Veloz Casas. 2 1/2" h. x 9" d.

Another interesting development in Mata Ortiz pottery is the combination of color enhanced by sgraffito designs. The butterfly design over the highly polished seed pot is an excellent example of this style, which is also evident in clay pots and plates that are not black. Adding the intricate etching over the color greatly enhances each design. These examples demonstrate the versatility of the Mata Ortiz artists.

We can expect to see many more innovations with regard to creating interesting patterns with colors. There is no limit to the designs that can be made with these techniques. Just look at the following pages and see what the potters are accomplishing with bright colors.

Black gunmetal polish with detailed and ornate traditional patterns painted in muted pink, green, gray and white. Signed Anastacio Villalobos. 7 ¾"h x 7 ¾"d.

Black polished pot with red traditional patterns on one half and green on the other. Signed Jesús Lozano. 5 ½"h x 6"d.

Black polished pot with red, blue and green etched and painted butterflies. Signed Karin Camacho. 3"h x 3 ¾"d.

Black polished pot with detailed, etched red and white butterflies and tree branches. Signed Elicena Cota. 4 ¼"h x 4"d.

Small black polished pot with multi-color designs. Signed RRR. 2 ¾"h x 2 ½"d.

Small black polished vase with multi-colors and step cut neck. Signed Elicena Cota. 4 ½"h x 2 ¼"d.

Special Shapes

There are many examples of Mata Ortiz pottery that have shapes far more interesting than a normal pot or vase. The Paquime' people, predecessors of the Mata Ortiz pottery phenomenon, created effigy pottery and other shapes. I think most of the unusually shaped pots probably had some utilitarian use and the effigy pots had spiritual meanings. It's interesting that the contemporary potters from the Mata Ortiz village create some similar shaped vessels and have used their innate talent and ability to shift the boundaries. When you view the many shapes created by modern Mata Ortiz potters you can decide for yourself how they compare to the ancient examples.

Fish effigy pot. Signed Cruz Renteria. 4' h. x 6 11/2" d.

Speckled beige pot with incised and painted butterfly design and a slanted, step-cut rim. Signed Angela Corona. 4" h. x 4 1/2" d.

Look at the fine examples of the unusual shaped pots on the following pages. Even though many of the shapes have been created in one form or another for many years, there are some new efforts to expand the craft. I think what separates the new pottery from some of the older examples is not the shape especially, but the intricacy of the construction. You can see in many of the photos that the carving is sharper and the lines are thinner and more symmetrical than pottery from earlier years. There are a few attempts to emulate shapes more common in Native American Pueblo pottery such as the wedding vase and the pottery canteen. The actual shapes are similar but the design work is typical Mata Ortiz style. These particular forms were introduced by traders from the north when they visited the Mata Ortiz village.

Black polished vase with gunmetal finish, long and fluted neck and flared, slanted rim. Signed Suzy D. Marinez. 7 1/4" h. x 3" d.

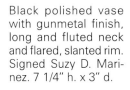

Black gunmetal polished vase with fluted neck and slanted rim. Signed Suzy D. Martinez. 9 1/2" h. x 6 1/2" d.

Red polished duck with black painted patterns. Signed José González. 6"h x 8 ½"d.

One of the most noticeable improvements in special shapes pottery is the "flowing" finishes on the top opening of some of the vases. Personally, I think this adds an entirely different dimension to the feel and expression of a piece. Imagine the same examples I've provided with just a straight finish on the opening, and I think you'll see what I mean about adding so much more to the pottery. These flared openings seem to draw the viewer to the pot and say "look at me, I am breaking barriers and improving on tradition."

I'm also impressed with new variations of the polished black pottery. There are many good examples of these pots with "melon" designs and relief carving of lizards and horned toads. I find the lifelike turtle pots and the pots with various animal heads carved in the form of bears, birds and fish to be a bridge between the old and new. All of these interesting designs are accomplished alongside magnificent polishing and in some instances geometric matte design work.

It is fascinating to see that the potters have respect and admiration for the past, yet search for ways to make new artistic expressions with their ever expanding talent. In fact, their creativity only serves to enhance the beauty of more traditional shapes.

Buff polished owl effigy with traditional black and red patterns. Signed Jorge Corona Guillén. 7"h x 6"d.

Buff polished effigy with red and black traditional designs. Signed Armando Rodríguez. 7 ½"h x 4 ½'d.

Black on black polished pot with fish handle top. Signed Paty Quezada. 4 ½"h. x 4 ½"d.

Black polished zoomorphic turtle pot.
Signed Estela López. 4"h. x 8"d.

Black polished pot with traditional green
patterns and formed fish top. Signed Olivia
Domínguez Rentería. 5"h. x 4"d.

Black polished zoomorphic turtle pot. Signed Estela López. 4"h. x 8"d.

Black on black polished pot with traditional painted patterns and raised lizards around the rim. Signed Reynaldo Quezada. 6 ½"h. x 9 ½"d.

Black gun metal polished vase with fluted neck and slanted rim.
Signed Suzy D. Martínez. 9 ½"h. x 6 ½"d.

Black polished vase with gun metal finish, long fluted neck and
flared, slanted rim. Signed Suzy D. Martínez. 7 ¼"h. x 3"d.

Fish effigy pot. Signed Cruz Rentería. 4"h. x 6 ½"d.

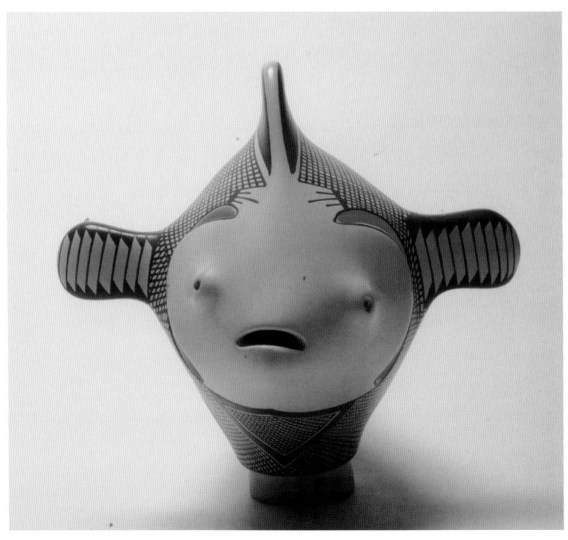

Beige polished canteen with painted black deer framed in black, red and green designs.
Signed Ángela Corona. 4 ¾"h. x 5"d.

Corrugated tan seed pot.
Signed Efrén Betancourt Pérez.
7 ¼"h. x 8"d.

Black polished ram effigy pot. Signed Estela de López. 5 ¼"h. x 3 ¾"d.

Speckled beige pot with incised and painted butterflies and a slanted step cut rim. Signed Ángela Corona. 4"h. x 4 ½"d.

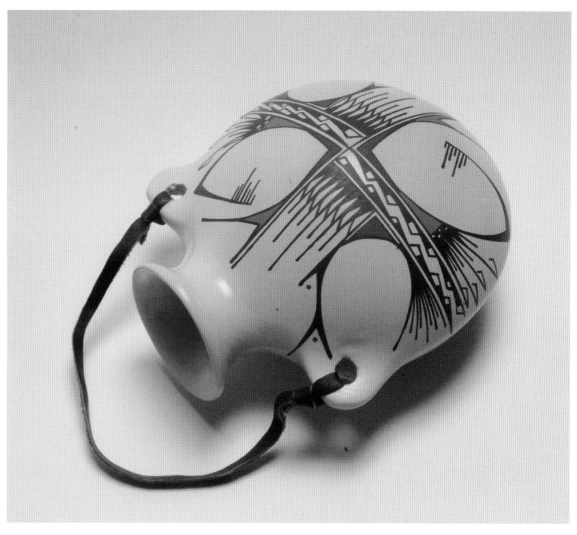

Beige polished canteen with traditional red, black and green painted patterns. Signed Ángela Corona. 4 ¾"h. x 5"d.

Beige plate with mimbres style rabbit designs in brown and red with finished back. Signed José Andrés Villalba H. 1 ½"h. x 9"d.

Fish effigy pot painted in traditional red and black patterns. Signed Jorge Corona Guillén. 5 ½"h. x 8"d.

Red wedding vase with red checker pattern and white dots. Signed Elsa Ledezma and Jorge Ponce. 6 ¼"h. x 5 ½"d.

Red polished wedding vase with black checker patterns and square openings and handle.
Signed Elsa Ledezma/Jorge Ponce. 5 ½"h. x 4"d.

Beige polished bowl with large black and red patterns and inset handles and apple coral stone.
Signed Gerardo Tena. 5"h. x 6"d.

Effigy pots. Signed Armando Rodríguez. 7 ½" h. x 4" d.

Owl effigy pot with red and black designs. Signed Jorge Corona Guillén. 7"h. x 5"d.

Black polished melon pot with two formed bear head handles. Signed Hector Quezada. 10"h. x 7"d.

Black polished melon pot with impressed neck.
Signed Héctor Ortega. 7 ½"h. x 8"d.

Beige polished pot with red lizard raised from the surface and
painted with traditional black patterns. Signed Olivia Domínguez
Rentería. 5"h. x 4 ½"d.

Black polished pot with
raised black matte horned
toad. Signed Martha M de
Quezada. 5 ½"h. x 6"d.

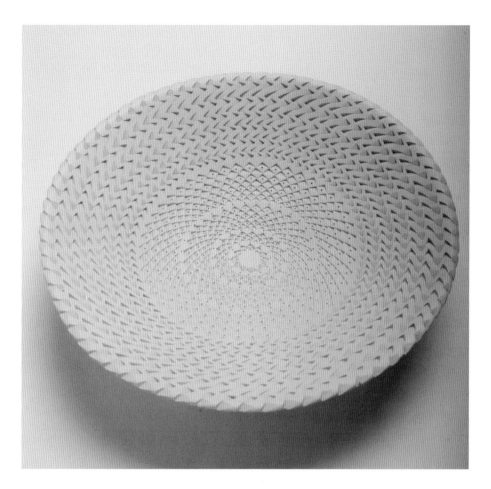

Beige corrugated bowl. Signed Mariano Quezada. 2 ½"h. x 12"d.

Beige corrugated seed pots with small fluted openings. Signed Fito Tena. 2"h. x 2 ½"d.

Tan corrugated seed pot with small fluted opening.
Signed Fito Tena. 3 ½"h. x 4 ½"d.

Beige pot with black and red checker and flower patterns. Signed Martha Martínez. 2 ½"h. x 4"d.

Beige polished effigy rabbit with red and black traditional patterns. Signed Nicolás Ortiz. 12"h. x 5"d.

Black polished zoomorphic turtle
pot. Signed Olivia Domínguez
Rentería. 4"h. x 7 ½"d.

Miniatures

More miniature Mata Ortiz pots are being made today than at any other time in the culture's relatively short history. Not only has the quantity increased but the quality has improved exponentially. There is also a move to bring some of the techniques used on the larger pots and create the same pots in miniature form. You'll see pots with the basic polychrome designs, pots with colors, pots with special shapes and pots with lids, corrugated pots, and pots with designs so small you'll wonder how the artist was able to achieve this perfection. The possibilities are endless.

Some of the most fun we had when putting this book together was gathering and photographing the miniatures. We were continually surprised at the delicacy and intricacy of these pots. It was impressive to see the similarities in the little pots, in relation to larger examples of the same techniques.

Miniature fine-line jar with a star-pattern lid.
Signed Cruz Renteria. 2" h. x 1" d.

Look closely at some of the finer painted examples of our miniature collection. Not only are the shapes exquisite but the designs are so small that they defy explanation. Whether it's the delicate rectangles with the dash of color inside or the finest lines you've ever seen, the work is beyond comparison. These superb examples show the innovation and ability to adapt Mata Ortiz pottery to any form.

It has been a special joy to participate in a small way with the introduction and proliferation of these tiny clay creations to various stores and collectors. We hope to see many more examples come our way so that we can continue to spread the word.

Three miniature, fine-line jars with turtle and knob-shaped lids.
Signed Cruz Renteria. 1 1/2" h. x 1 1/2" d. and 2" h. x 1 1/2" d.

Beige seed pots with green, red and brown star patterns.
Signed Nellie Reyes. 1"h. x 2 ½"d.

Mixed clay seed pots. Signed Nellie Reyes. 1"h. x 1 ½"d.

Mixed clay pots with insect and traditional patterns. Signed Manuela Olivas. 1 ¼"h. x 1 ¾"d.

Mixed clay pots with traditional red and black designs. Signed Manuela Olivas. 1 3/8"h. x 1 ¾"d.

Small egg shaped green seed pot with black lightning pattern and white egg shaped seed pot with painted insects. Signed Lupita Glez (González). 2 ¾"h. x 2"d.

Buff polished pot with red and black checker and diamond patterns with flattened top. Signed Rubén Ponce. 4"h. x 5"d.

Black melon pots with white feather patterns. Signed Carmen Veloz. 1 3/8"h. x 2 3/8"d.

Gray, green, red, and buff corrugated seed pots. Signed Fito Tena. 1"h. x 1 1/8"d.

Mini fine line jars with turtle and knob lids. Signed Cruz Rentería.
1 ½"h. x 1 ½"d. and 2"h. x 1 ½"d.

Mini fine line jar with star pattern lid.
Signed Cruz Rentería. 2"h. x 1"d.

Red polished vase with black checker pattern. Signed Guadalupe Ledezma.
Smaller size 3 7/8"h. x 3 1/8"d.

Beige polished miniature pots with varied red and black painted traditional patterns, and animal and insect designs. Signed Carmen Veloz. 1"h. x 1 ¾"d.

Beige polished plates with incised and painted bees, hummingbirds, rabbits and squirrels.
Signed Luz Elva Gutiérrez. ¾"h. x 4 ½"d.

Small beige polished vase with detailed, repetitive patterns. Signed Cruz Rentería. 4"h. x 2 ½"d.

Various corrugated seed pots. Signed Fito Tena. 2"h. x 2 ½"d. to 3 ½"h. x 4"d.

Miniature seed pots with red and black painted star patterns. Signed Nellie Reyes. ¾"h. x 1 ¾"d. and 1 ¼"h. x 2"d.

Red seed pots with beige traditional patterns. Signed Avelina Corona. 2"h. x 3"d.

Black and red polished pots with checker patterns.
Signed Guadalupe Ledezma. 2"h. x 3 ½"d.

Red polished pots with red and black checker
design and etched ants. Signed Yoly Ledezma.
Smaller size 3 ¼"h. x 4 ¼"d.

Beige seed pots painted with black and red traditional patterns. Signed Carmen Veloz. ¾"h. x 2 ¼"d.

Miniature fish seed pot. Signed Raúl Jurado Domínguez. ¾"h. x 1 ½"d.

Egg shaped insect seed pots. Signed Lupita Glez (González). 2"h. x 1 ¾"d.

Glossary

Corrugated- a ridge and groove pattern on the surface
Effigy- a representation of a person or animal that could have spiritual meaning
Graphite polish technique- copier toner mixed with diesel fuel applied to the surface and rubbed with a smooth rock
Matte Finish- lacking or deprived of luster or gloss
Oxidation firing- baking pottery with oxygen present
Oxides- binary compounds of oxygen with a more electropositive element
Polychrome- relating to decoration in several colors
Reduction firing- baking pottery without oxygen
Relief carving- design cut with a sharp outline
Stone polished- made smooth or glossy with a rock

Bibliography

Lowell, Susan and Jim Hills, Jorge Quintana Rodriguez, Michael Wisner, *The Many Faces of Mata Ortiz*, Tucson: Rio Nuevo Publishers, 1999.
Parks, Walter P. *The Miracle of Mata Ortiz*. The Coulter Press, 1993.
Powell, Melissa S. *Secrets of Casas Grandes*, Santa Fe: Museum of Indian Arts and Culture/ Laboratory of Anthropology, 2006.

Personal Interview:
Susman, Nancy, Museum of Arts and Culture, Santa Fe, New Mexico.

Index of Artists